THE DEADLY MOSQUITO

THE DISEASES THESE TINY INSECTS CARRY

HEALTH BOOK FOR KIDS
CHILDREN'S DISEASES BOOKS

BABY PROFESSOR
EDUCATION KIDS

Speedy Publishing LLC

40 E. Main St. #1156

Newark, DE 19711

www.speedypublishing.com

Copyright 2018

In this book, we're going to talk about mosquitoes and the diseases they carry. So, let's get right to it!

When you think of dangerous animals, you usually think about large animals with sharp teeth like lions or sharks.

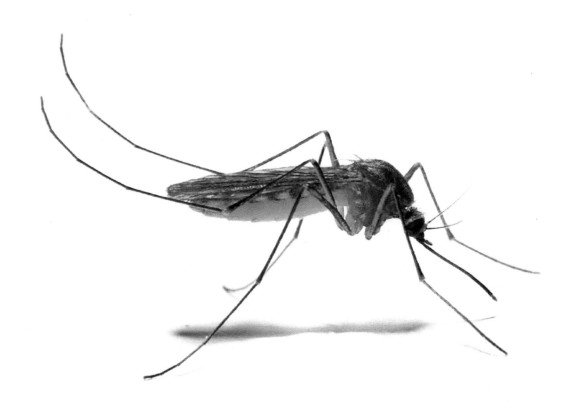

However, some of the animals that are the deadliest to humans are insects. Of these deadly insects, mosquitoes are the ones that cause the most human deaths every year.

AEDES AEGYPTI MOSQUITO

Mosquitoes are very tiny insects. They are usually between 0.125 and 0.75 inches in length and they only weigh about 0.00009 ounces. They are invertebrates, which simply means they don't have skeletons. They seem harmless enough.

When you're at an outdoor barbecue or you go for a hike in the woods, there are sometimes swarms of mosquitoes. If you are bitten by a mosquito, the bite leaves an itchy red welt on your arm or wherever you've been bitten.

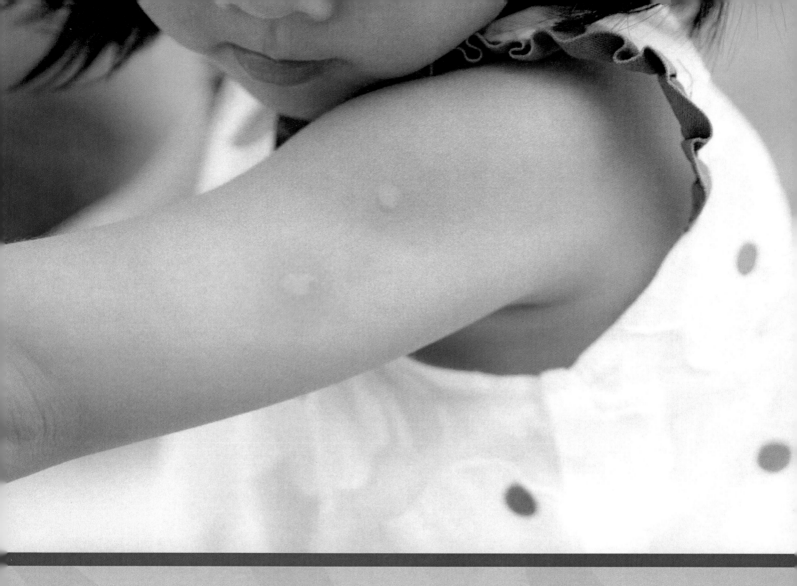

The red bump is an allergic reaction to the substances the mosquito has discharged into your blood.

You might put some salve on the bite to ease the itching and not give it another thought. Most mosquito bites are harmless and will just cause some irritation for a day or two. However, some mosquito bites are deadly because mosquitoes can transmit diseases, both to other animals and to humans.

MOSQUITOES SUCK BLOOD

Mosquitoes find their victims by detecting carbon dioxide that is being exhaled. They can also sense body odors and temperature as well as movement. So, if you are running through the woods on a hot, sultry day, you are a prime target for a mosquito bite.

Male mosquitoes don't bite. Only the females have the needed body parts to suck blood out of their victims. They bite using a proboscis. They push two small tubes into their victims' skin.

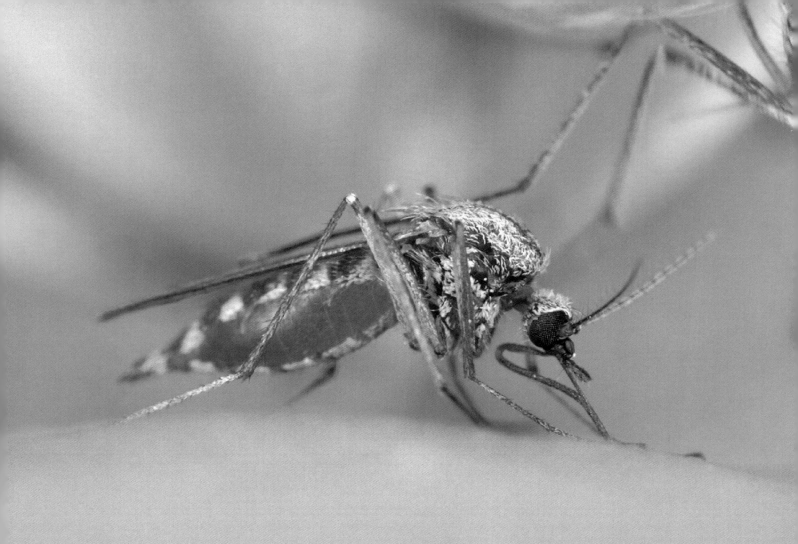

One tube carries a special enzyme to stop the blood from clotting so that it will continue to flow out. The other tube is used to suck up the blood.

Surprisingly, they don't use the blood to nourish themselves. Instead, the blood is used as a protein source for the production of their eggs. Both male mosquitoes and female mosquitoes consume nectars from flowers and plants for their food source.

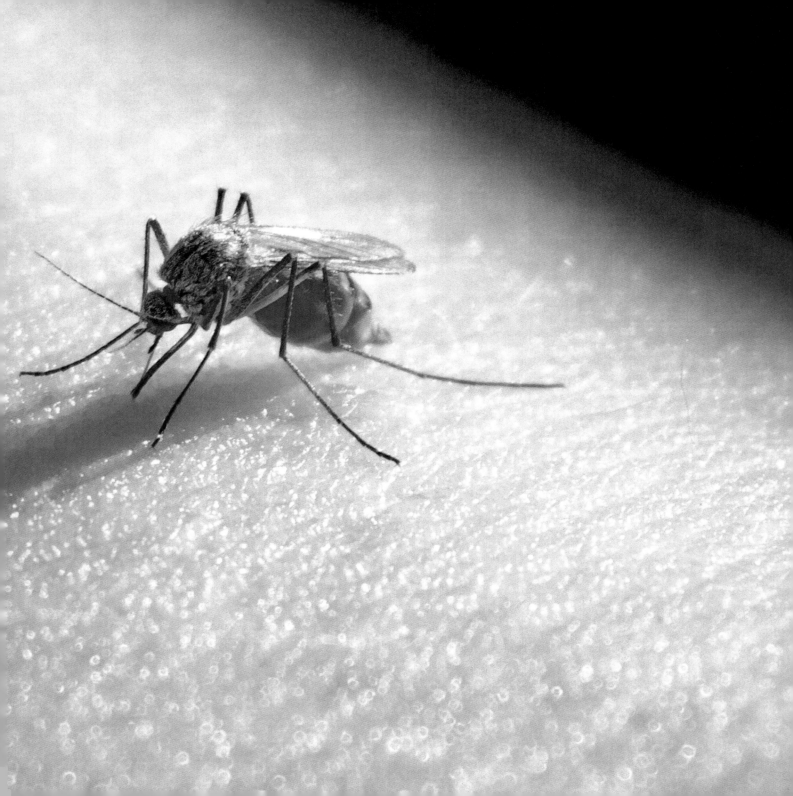

MOSQUITOES BREED IN STAGNANT WATER

CONTROLLING THE POPULATION OF MOSQUITOES

Mosquitoes breed in standing water so it's important to get rid of these types of water sources to control the spread of mosquitoes. There are also insecticides designed to get rid of mosquitoes.

ENVIRONMENTAL HEALTH WORKERS ARE
FOGGING FOR MOSQUITO CONTROL

Unfortunately, these two ways are not enough to control the huge population of mosquitoes worldwide and the rate of infection by mosquitoes has been increasing.

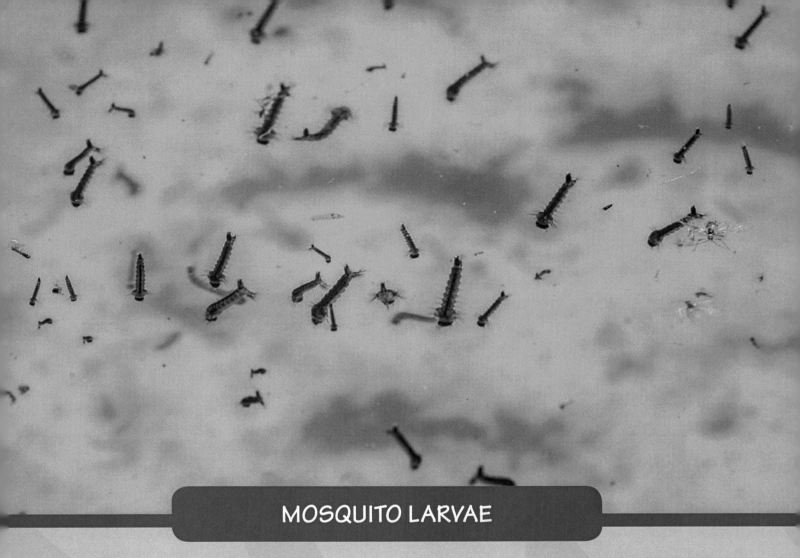

MOSQUITO LARVAE

Many scientists believe that the changing of the world's temperature due to global warming will actually increase the populations of mosquitoes and make their range even more extensive.

FROG EATING A MOSQUITO

There would definitely be an impact on the environment if people eliminated all forms of mosquitoes. Thousands of different types of animals use mosquitoes as a source of food. Birds and bats eat them, so do dragonflies and frogs.

HOW DO MOSQUITOES CARRY DISEASES?

When a mosquito bites an animal or person that has a disease, it gets infected and the parasite that causes the disease goes into the mosquito's body.

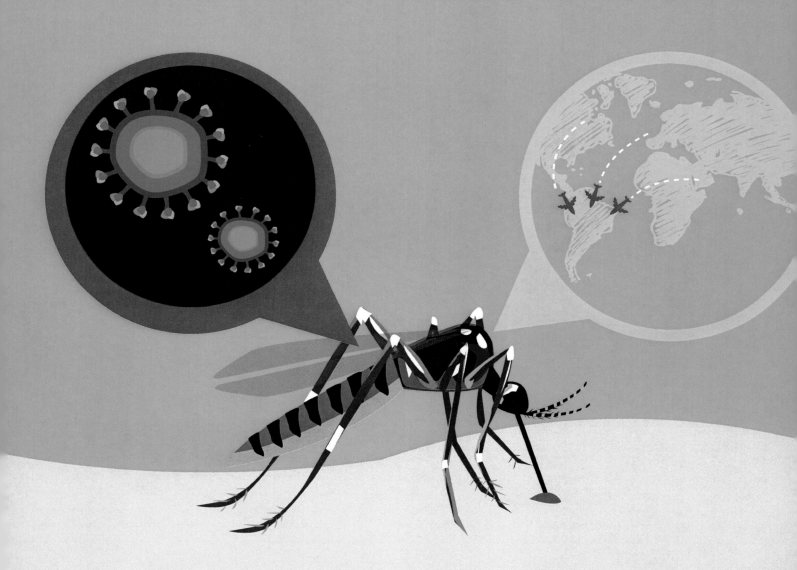

MOSQUITO CARRYING ZIKA VIRUS

Danger!

When the mosquito bites her victim, the parasites are carried through her saliva and enter the victim through his or her blood stream. The parasites don't cause much, if any, harm to the mosquito, but the victim can become severely ill or die from the disease that the mosquito carried.

WHICH TYPES OF MOSQUITOES ARE DEADLY TO HUMANS?

There are over 3,000 different species of mosquitoes, but only three of these species are responsible for most of the deadly diseases that they carry. It's actually not the mosquitoes themselves that are deadly. It's the parasites that the mosquitoes carry in their bodies that cause the diseases.

DANGEROUS AEDES AEGYPTI MOSQUITO ON HUMAN SKIN

Luckily, humans are not their preferred victims.

Mosquitoes would prefer to bite birds, cattle, and horses more than humans. Despite this, according to the United States Center for Disease Control, over one million people around the world die each year as a result of infectious mosquito bites. Most of the deaths are caused by malaria.

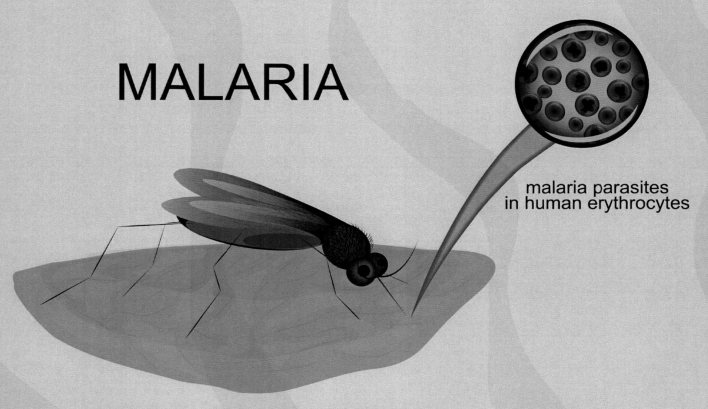

MALARIA

malaria parasites in human erythrocytes

a mosquito of the genus Anopheles

ANOPHELES MOSQUITO

The three types of mosquitoes that carry the deadliest diseases are:

ANOPHELES

This type of mosquito is the only type that is known to carry the deadly disease of malaria. They also carry elephantiasis, also called filariasis, as well as encephalitis.

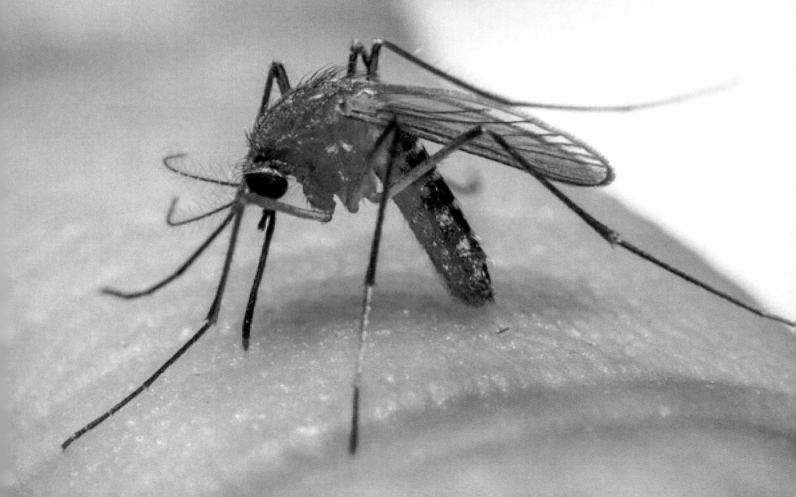

ANOPHELES

CULEX

In addition to carrying the diseases of filariasis and encephalitis as the Anopheles mosquitoes do, Culex mosquitoes also carry West Nile virus.

AEDES

Aedes mosquitoes carry encephalitis. They also carry yellow fever and dengue fever.

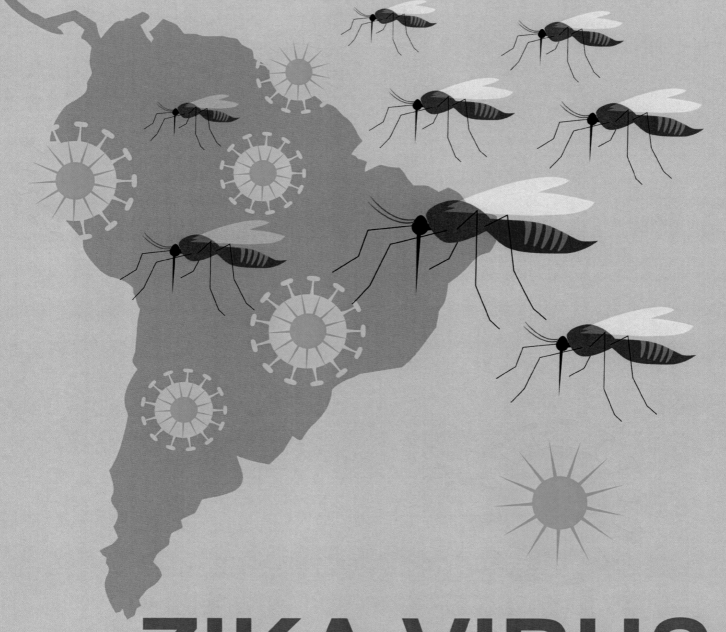

ZIKA VIRUS

DISEASES THAT MOSQUITOES CARRY

Here are some of the deadly diseases that mosquitoes carry.

ZIKA VIRUS

The Zika virus came from infected monkeys and has been transmitted to humans from mosquitoes. The types of mosquitoes that carry this virus are the Aedes aegypti and the Aedes albopictus, which is also called the Asian tiger mosquito.

The mosquito bites an infected monkey or other primate and then carries the disease inside its body.

Once it bites a person and infects him or her, then that person can also infect someone else through sexual contact. This virus poses a special danger to the unborn children of women who are pregnant. It can result in a birth defect, which is called microcephaly. Babies born with this defect have smaller heads than normal babies and as a result they may have mental and physical disabilities.

Zika Virus causes microcephaly

Zika Virus can be transmitted from a pregnant mother to her fetus.

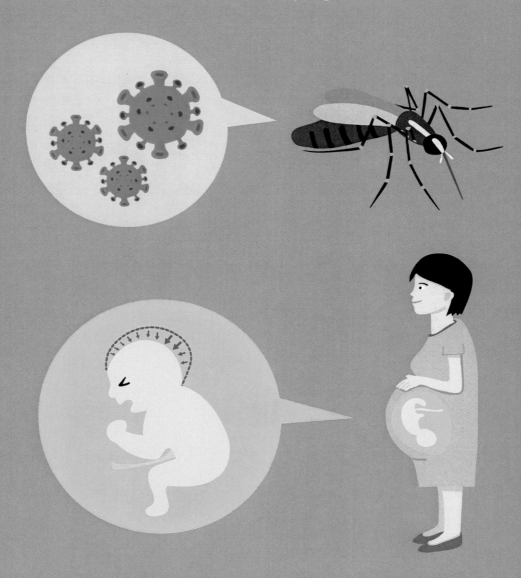

MOSQUITO REPELLENT SPRAY

More than 80% of the people who become infected don't realize that they are carriers of the virus because the symptoms are similar to the symptoms of a common cold. The symptoms include a low fever and red eyes. Pain in the joints and rash are other common symptoms of the Zika virus.

At the current time, there isn't any way to treat or prevent this disease except to prevent bites from mosquitoes by using mosquito repellent. The disease has spread to most continents and over the last few years has spread to North and South America.

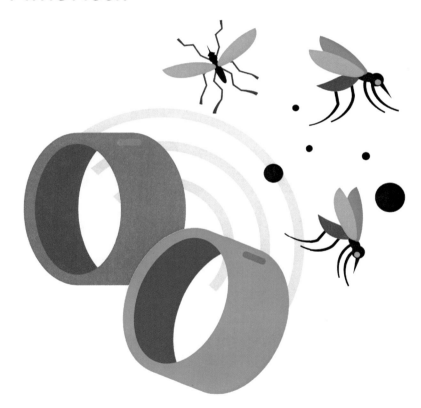

MOSQUITO REPELLING BRACELETS

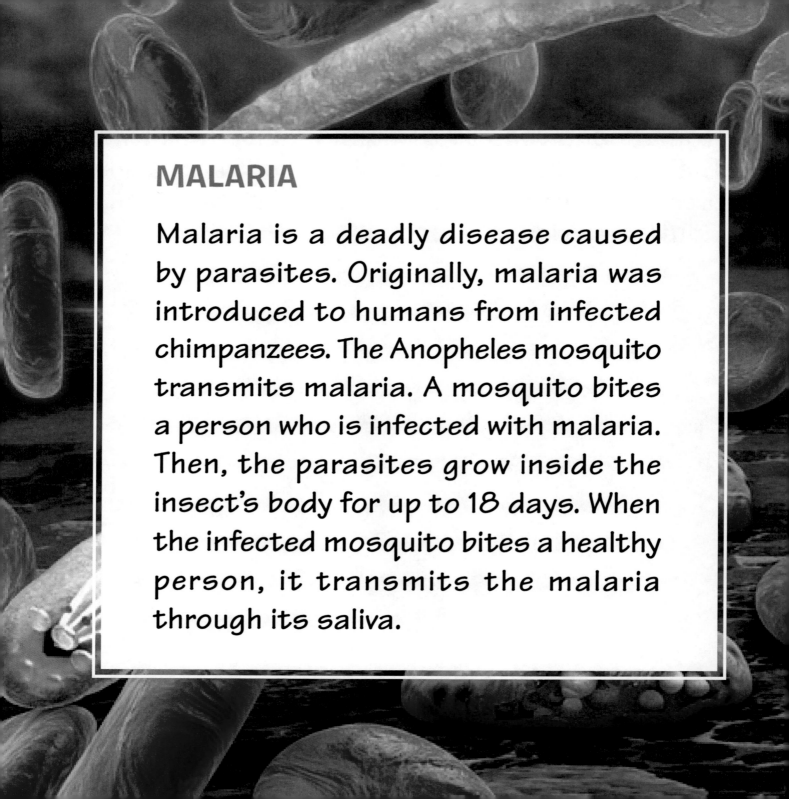

MALARIA

Malaria is a deadly disease caused by parasites. Originally, malaria was introduced to humans from infected chimpanzees. The Anopheles mosquito transmits malaria. A mosquito bites a person who is infected with malaria. Then, the parasites grow inside the insect's body for up to 18 days. When the infected mosquito bites a healthy person, it transmits the malaria through its saliva.

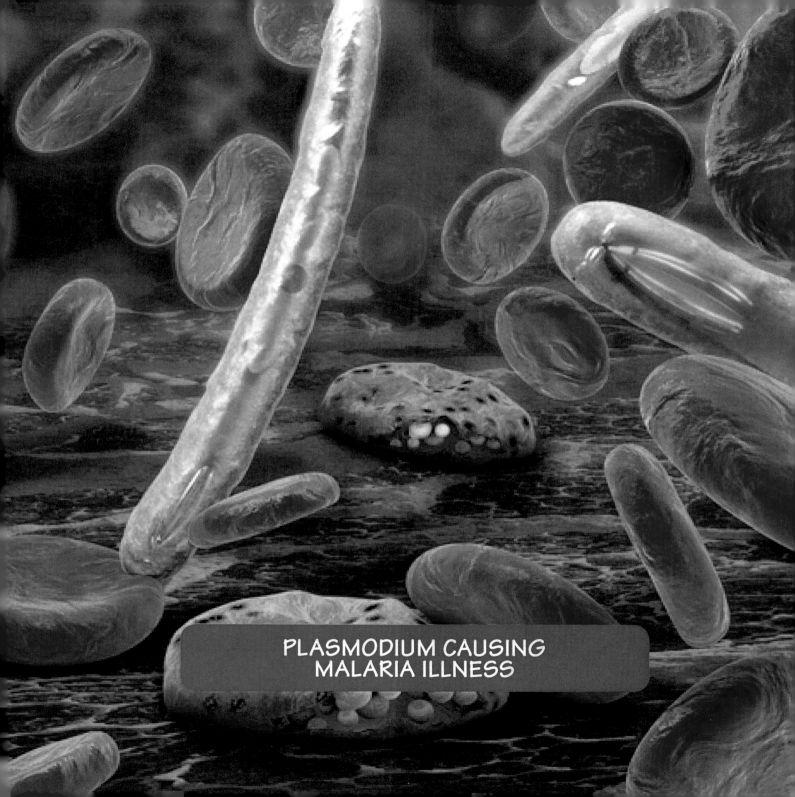

PLASMODIUM CAUSING
MALARIA ILLNESS

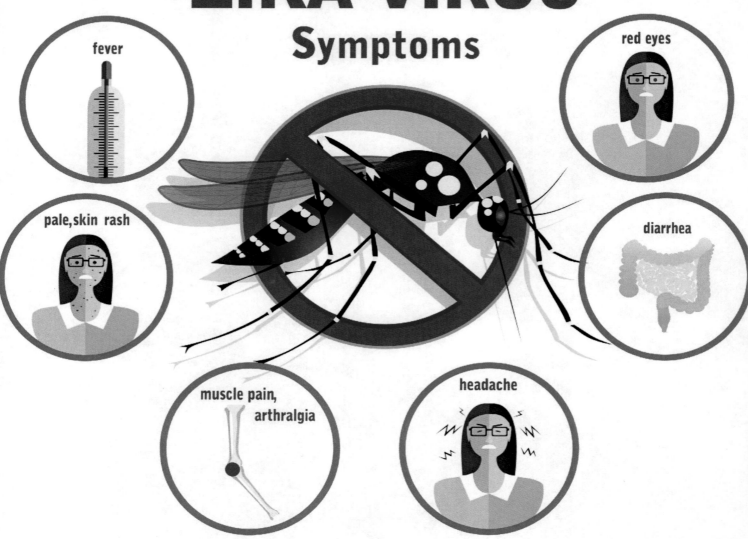

When the parasites get inside a person's body, they travel to the liver. There, they begin to multiply. Next, they travel to the person's blood and begin to destroy the red blood cells. At this point, the individual begins to get very sick with fevers, sweating, and chills. He or she starts experiencing severe headaches and other symptoms that can be mistaken for the flu. If malaria goes untreated, it can result in the failure of the kidneys and death. Fortunately, there are drugs to combat malaria, such as quinine. These drugs work by attacking and killing the parasites within the blood.

WEST NILE VIRUS

The West Nile virus is transmitted when a Culex mosquito bites a bird that is infected with the virus. Then, after the virus penetrates the mosquito's body, it transmits the virus through its saliva when it bites a human.

West Nile Virus

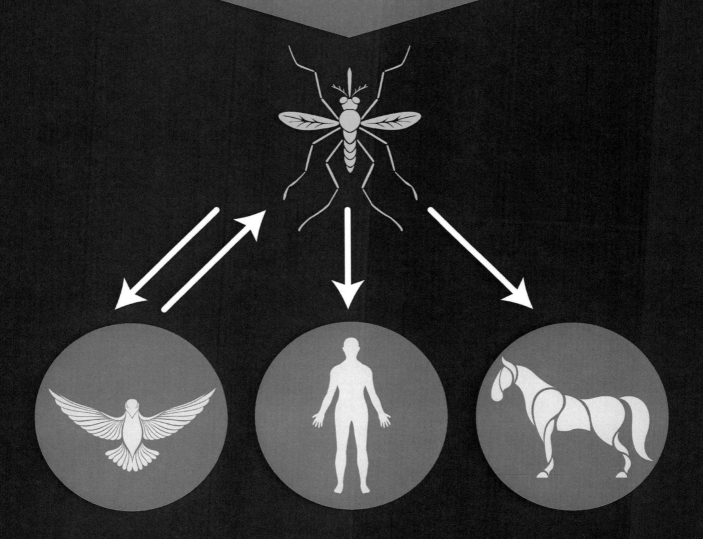

Out of 150 people who are infected with the virus, only one will develop severe symptoms. People over the age of 50 are the most at risk for developing a more serious illness. In the cases that are severe, the virus develops in the blood and is carried to the brain tissue. It starts to affect the nervous system and it causes encephalitis, which is inflammation of the tissue in the brain.

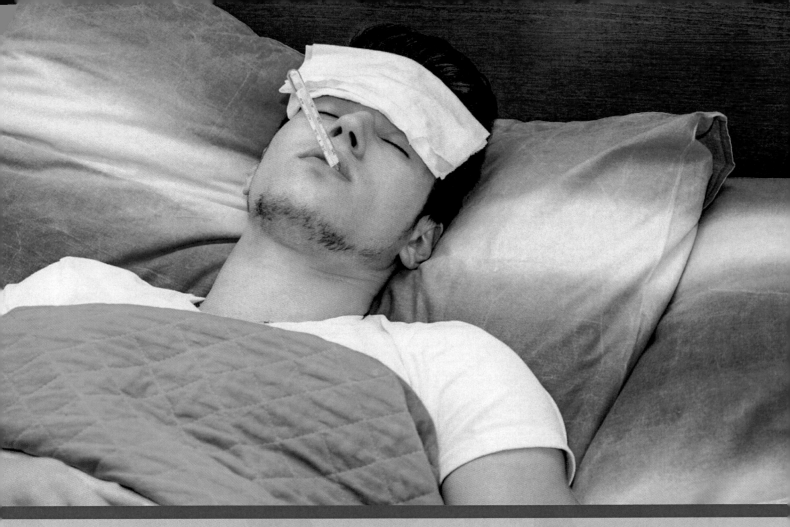

If the virus gets to this stage, the infected person gets a very high fever, severe headaches, a stiff neck, and swelling of the lymph nodes. As the disease continues, it can lead to convulsions as well as coma or death.

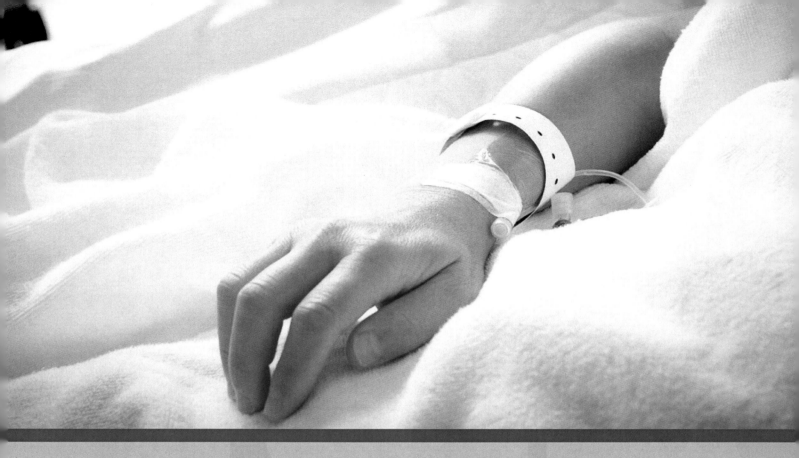

Even if someone survives the convulsions or coma, he or she would more than likely have permanent damage to the nervous system. There isn't any treatment currently available to combat West Nile virus although there is some evidence that people who are infected and survive become immune to the disease.

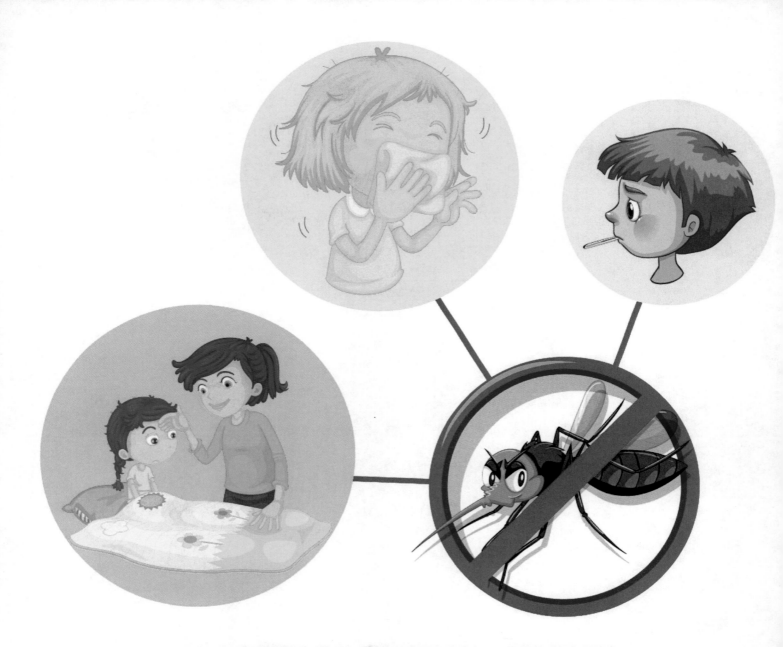

GETTING BIT BY A MOSQUITO
CAN MAKE YOU SICK!

DENGUE FEVER

Originally, dengue fever came from monkeys sometime between 100-800 years ago. Today, over 100 million adults and children get sick with dengue fever every year. It is especially common in hot, tropical climates such as in Africa, Southeast Asia, and the tropical areas of the Western Hemisphere. The disease is spread by Aedes mosquitoes. A mosquito bites an infected person and then, within a week, the mosquito's bites will transmit the virus to a healthy person.

The infected person suffers from a high fever as well as severe headaches and joint pain. Rashes and pain in the eyes are other common symptoms. If the person's fever lasts more than a week and the victim has bruises and episodes of bleeding, then it is a sign that he or she has hemorrhagic fever, which results in death about 5% of the time. There isn't a cure for this disease.

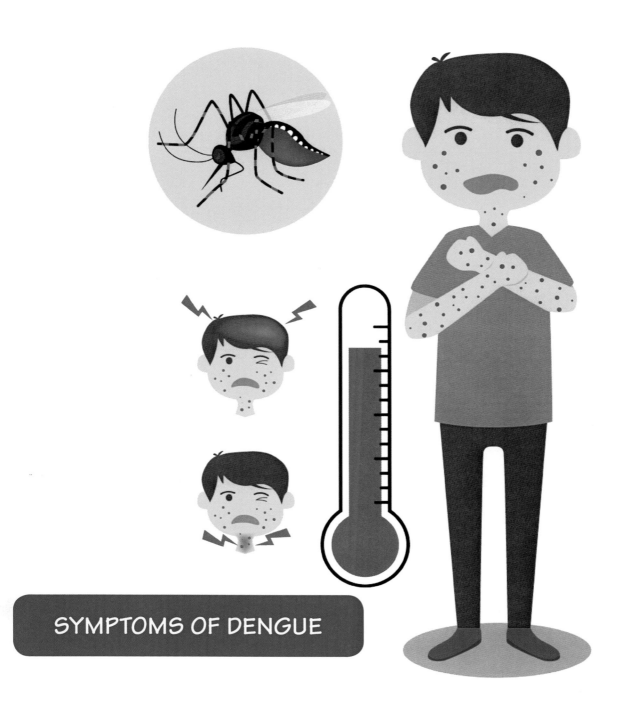

SYMPTOMS OF DENGUE

SICK PATIENT

YELLOW FEVER

Yellow fever, like dengue, is carried by the Aedes species. In fact, the Aedes aegypti is called the yellow fever species. After a mosquito bites an infected person and transmits it to another person, there is an incubation period of about six days. Then, the person will exhibit chills and nausea. Sometimes the illness seems to go away but then comes back with nosebleeds as well as vomiting with blood and severe abdominal pain. There is a vaccine for yellow fever and travelers going to areas where yellow fever is common are advised to get it.

SUMMARY

Mosquitoes are the deadliest animals on Earth. A few species of these tiny insects carry a host of diseases, which injure and kill millions of people every year. There are very few treatments for these diseases so it's best to use mosquito repellant and try to avoid being bitten.

Now that you've read about mosquitoes and the diseases they carry, you may want to read about other deadly insects in the Baby Professor book Crawl, Bite & Sting! Deadly Insects | Insects for Kids Encyclopedia | Children's Bug & Spider Books.

Visit

BABY PROFESSOR
EDUCATION KIDS

www.BabyProfessorBooks.com

to download Free Baby Professor eBooks
and view our catalog of new and exciting
Children's Books